RABBIT

When poetry is the centre of your life the strength of some poets will get fixed in the orbit of your day, their poems settled into the memory of mind and body. Sophie Robinson is one of my absolute favourites, her lines returning to me, visceral, unsettling, exacting, and stunning! If you read one book of poems this year, let it be this! She's a gateway drug, keeping you wanting all books of poetry to be as genius to make part of your waking life.

— CA Conrad, author of *While Standing in Line for Death*

RABBIT
SOPHIE ROBINSON

BOILER HOUSE PRESS

I

II

III

for my Mum & Dad

I

the candy here is hard & filled & there is nothing i love more
than to be treasured. if nobody's watching i just do nothing: lie down
don't hardly breathe, keep my face in careful stillness not to crease
its cute forgettability. the world is full of edible munchkins & it is my
    life's work
to work out how to stay creamy on the inside, how not to sour myself
up with little nips of this or that or otherwise cut holes in myself thru
    which
to be seen. i must learn to love what i cannot know: the wide bleached
    anus
on a porn blog, the insane demands of toddlers, the desire for
    moderation or
slimness of affection, the reasons lovers leave, the trash my cat brings
    back,
the crack of footsteps in the woods at night, why the killer kills.
i learn it all the hard way but fwiw
i would never snap the rabbit's neck again
i would rewind i would keep it every time

in paris we were always waiting for rome to burn & when you say *voilà* what you really mean is *don't look at this, i have already looked for you, i am telling you to look in order that you do not.* so it goes round in circles like this looking & not looking in a place on fire, in a long thin line of fire running as a vein

barbara streisand called she wants her songs back & other indignities, falling together forever off a mountain of regret. in london we were always waiting for paris to burn with the heat of itself as we sat in our damp selves. the rain pours. meryl streep called, she wants her kids back & everybody crying in a line, sobbing into the next person's shoulders & me at the end, back sodden with tears & nobody to cry on anyway, even though the whole thing was my idea

tracey emin called she wants these self-pitying affectations back & i can't pay her. not this month. we are all going to die soon. i wish we had sex more. if i lie on my back & you lie on your front & we are in the same bed is that sex. draw a line between your eyes & down the middle of your nose & split your lips & there you have it. light a match. your face is a mountain in case you hadn't guessed & i like to think i carved it

all the animals here have big & heavy heads & i am fucking sick of their hydrocephalic tumbling slicking back the skin to reveal flowers blooming in the folds & now everybody's calling to say they love you & i should stop talking –

raw raw raw raw raw raw raw raw raw raw that is how a dog goes
that his how a dog goes boom in the night that is how a dog slides
sideways that is how a dog lies down in the grass & loafes & dies like
the bad dead dog it really is inside its orgied guts & this is how we do
it: in out in out this is how we move inside the dog space this is how
we are inside the dog i am the dog head with my head inside the dog
you are the dog end with your end inside the dog we are a pantomime
dog & this is how we do it: left right left right that is how we walk like
the sick dogs we are that is how we fuck ourselves inside out & our
fur turns to mush this is how we love ourselves with suffering this is
how we think of something to make us cry on purpose this is how we
be brave & glass over like a sad dog's eyes this is how we eat our own
shit & sing with a mouthful all night long: raw raw raw raw raw raw
raw raw raw raw this is how we know ourselves & this is how we hate
each other this is how we sound when we speak each other's language
& how your pussy tastes on a hard day's night i like to suffer it's good
for us & makes us wet with pride or raw with longing pulling at the
leash i might die i might lie down & die you can dog me in the park
& i won't let it lie i'd screw you five thousand times & still be happy
in my mummy skin in my daggy dogskin in my foxfur mangy woof
woof jacket. my skin is my life jacket my skin has a hole in it my hole
is round & red my hole is a dog's head i will die forever in my sick dog
head i will lol forever in my total bowl of meat i will lol with my hole
wide open i will lol all night to the tune of my howl o i will place you
in my snout & sing you all over i will raw myself all up & down inside
you lover forever

PARTY

the cat is sick. i'm dead tired again, am nobody's friend today. same old bloodlines calling back. echo.

you nobody's daughter. you die just to call it in. but wait: everybody's on the shore. they threw a party for you that you would be ok. that you would not be too drunk to go to this time.

at this party nobody cries. at this party nobody is bored or afraid. people dance & talk all nite people tangle their ankle in sea fronds until their toes go blue. the quiet wired ghosts that bring the ships in. a banner in the sky: *it doesn't matter it doesn't matter it doesn't matter that you feel this way.*

no birds in the trees no people no weeping no clawing back your hair
no plunging into black lakes no making a sport of yourself no sigh in
the night no photograph of fun no sunray splaying out of your head
no grass between your toes no weeping no clawing back the time
no garden no yard no park no reserve no train no bus no car no taxi
no oyster no pearl no bucket of sand no heart no lungs no babies
no buddies nobody on the streets nobody in the houses nobody in
the factories nobody in the shops nobody in the offices no weeping
no clawing back the cash nothing on the television nobody picking
up the phone no father no sister no mother no brother no gf no bf
nothing on the television nobody picking up the phone no tanning
no manicure no waiting no dreaming no blood no carpets no rugs no
blankets of skin no moon no stars no shine shine no mountains no
ribs no sticky darkness no day no drifting no woodland fantasy no
herd no murder no nest no egg no rhino no rhinestone no cowboy
no milkmaid no alpine air no toxic shock no burn nothing on the
television nobody picking up the phone no cancer no tumour no
surgeon no vet no door to the past no white light no deadly vision
no school no country no loving arm no worm no beetle no losing
hand nobody in the banks nobody in the libraries nobody on the
radio nobody on the road nobody in the town square nothing on the
television nobody picking up the phone no crushing no kissing no
anal no fisting no welts upon your back no gull no squaw no macho
walk no swagger say hello to the past the future the present danger
nobody to hold you nobody to say goodbye nobody baking in the
earth's red sun nobody falling down the earth's wide cracks nothing
on the television nobody picking up the phone no sunburn no blister
no happy life no cracks in your head no bucket of blood no gurgling
baby no spider in his crib no omen no coughing up your lungs no
body beside you no bitter coffee thrill no fearful lurch of guts no pills
no coke no goblet of wine no 2-4-1 plastix no weeping actors no calf no
lamb no suckling babes no blowjob no swimming pool no pull of tide
no medic no pastor no visionary poet no police no police no police
on the street no weeping no clawing back the land no air no breath

no lips in the night no perfume no gemstone no love letter no ship no
rig no lifeguard no plague no cure no flies upon your face no majik
no ritual no ghost beside your bed no mummy doesn't love you no
herald angel no saint no body on the pyre no surf no moss no lichen
no tree roots to wrap around your feet your throat no storm no neon
ball of light no arms to shield your eyes no world at the end of itself
no witness nothing on the television nobody picking up the phone
nothing on the television nobody picking up the phone nothing on
the television nobody picking up the phone nothing on the television
nobody picking up the phone nothing on the television nobody
picking up the phone nothing on the television nobody picking up
the phone nothing on the television nobody picking up the phone
nothing on the television nobody picking up the phone nothing on
the television nobody picking up the phone

I HATE FLOWERS

all i want is sinking ships
all i want is ships under water
trains under water

cars dropped from ships into water
trains carriage by carriage like links
of sausage dragging each other under

transport is so playful without weight
or purpose – metal bubbled laughter
a whole sea of metal and salt

i don't want to be taken anywhere
i want the traffic to stay still
i want the future lost & rusted

all i want is everything
underwater forever rendered
in scum

i want everything looking
like a shitty picture
of what it used to be

sun set down train window the sky shines like a thick lake & the old
clouds foam off north sea to faux a mountaintop like when we looked
for that night stream to swim in up so high we drew our breath in
pacy blades left dry & swimming only in clouds & that one stalinist
monument so beige it was cut from that sky & flowered shrines to
nobodies we found in clumps & did not tell & the man we saw crying
on a stump nearby & did not tell were driven lower & lower until our
ears popped & none of us talked until we reached the cold hotel & now
the coal train drives me high & i take the heat i'm the nobody & you're
the man who shrined me you sit on your stump & cry now go as the
trees to the lake you won't come close now no

<3

> jagged are names and not our creatures
> — *Veronica Forrest-Thompson*

i wish i had a better name to be called by like you might call a dog at
  a lake and she would surely turn
& i could eat your name for days: i would gladly bow my head o as the
  ploughman to the plough
& become the machine that made me that gave me my name my job
  (& what would i be called then)
for now i sit & wait in boots i made myself & laced in faith on better
  days than this with better names
& all & thinking on the names that trump other names & who wears
  them; how for example when you search
for yourself you don't always find what you're looking for or say your
  name & feel like a stranger
at the bank with your wad of cash for rent or at the park you stop
  when called to find a pup called sophie
chasing down a human you don't know. do you have a problem in
  your life? no.
buddha says: look on the internet & you will surely find one i mean
  a problem.
i had 107 problems & i named them all to keep them safe (each of
  them is called "<3")
& then i kissed them on the back and sides, i brushed their hair
  & called them my baby diamonds.
buddha says: name your price. so i named my price sophie & she
  is high & heavy, she is surely gold, but now
i want to call my price better i want to make my price a price a dog
  would pay. besides
you can call my price by any name and she will come just the same.
like dogs we neglect our work & lie on soft carpet and laugh and rofl
  about
to the tune of the internet & shed our love

all upon & around our bumbling manchild that we made & named.
you can say eat the cake & you can even eat it
but you can't say anna mae & no you can't turn her. how stupid & crazy
     to always have to say everything
so much, to have to tell people not to hit it up or be a fucking joker,
     to have to always be the one
to say no & then the long walk back to womanhood so obvious and
     boring to you
so you make up names & say you are anything
or write some awkward long-limbed poem just to remember that
you have a clit. if you turn the head of my dog she will surely come but
my cat does not come when i call he doesn't come anywhere at all
but stays home all day shagging blankets or crying on the roof
     & waiting
for my face at the window. buddha says: do you get naked in the
     distant thunder. no sir.
i keep my clothes on so my pets will know me so my poems will
     know me.

neil armstrong was dead. amy winehouse was dead. adrienne rich was dead. michael jackson was dead. chris marker was dead. shulamith firestone was dead. the streets were empty. the houses were empty like everyone had gone shopping except for us. you dove down under & came up with a big fat pearl between your legs & kissed me & killed the wanting before my wet eyes.

in your actress times you'd always play the rougher parts entrance the
lives of the stupid throats of ordinary people & i'd be some posh bitch
laying down the law & then i'd go home & wank w/out coming until i
fell asleep thinking about the echo of your laugh on a sound stage or
the curve of your swollen thigh thru rippling or bubbled water –

o sometimes i'm smiling like a kid in my knickers. my spandex & my
glue gun. my hunger stripes across me. my face of painted leather. my
ruddiness my boozelashed bits. the raw earth of my home the pink
tough ridges of my padding heels. lifelong softness. muscle me into
feeling, start up the piano –

ok so stupid feelings
will take their hold
at this moment
& every. like the whole
time i say i'm anything but
angry i'm covering or feeling
sorry enough for you to pretend
i wasn't
full of rage
from the beginning.
five years old a boy
touched my future cunt
i mean just some flesh
but i knew
he touched it & i thought a while
came into school & decided
no sir
him face down on a table
& me face to face
with my sad divorcing parents
getting told
i lacked discipline
& should stay quieter.
i'm twenty nine now &
since i was five i have been
sexually assaulted many times.
first time: bad boyfriend
in the woods.
second time: bad boyfriend
in his room.
third time: some boy
got his dick out
at the trocadero
millenium eve

forced my head
onto it
& i had lied
about where i was
& when i started
running i didn't stop
until i was on the train
home & watched the fireworks
thru the window bursting
thru my chest quietly
minus a fistful of hair.
fourth time: my drink
got spiked. fifth time: my drink
got spiked. sixth time: my drink
got spiked. seventh time: got
groped. eighth time: got groped.
ninth time: drink got spiked.
tenth: late & drunk & high & lost
two guys with hands
shoved up my skirt & thru
my tights & into my pants & in
there like really inside me
all my winter wasted
months on pills & they tore
my only coat & i was always cold.
eleventh time: a guy felt
me up at a bus stop
for a long time & i cried
& stayed still the whole
time he was doing it.
twelfth time: a guy felt me
up on the tube & i just felt
mild anger like almost
nothing. thirteenth time: a guy
put his hand between
my legs as i was walking
home from work & the police

drove me thru south london
to find the guy
but every guy was the guy
& nobody got lost
but me. fourteenth time:
a bar in stoke newington.
i was high on coke & new love
& in my best leather skirt.
i told him: don't touch me ·
& he touched me again
& then i said i said
don't touch me. he told me
to go fuck myself
& he smacked me
in the face
hard
with the back of his hand
& his ring cut
my cheek
& everyone there
more than 100 people
i guess
did nothing:
did not help
or act as witness
or stop anything
that happened.
i am up to number
twenty or so now
but i just really can't
be bothered to tell you
any more about my times
as a boring or bored or hurt
person in that way
other than to say:
it did hurt
most of the time

or does
& i have not reached
the last time
this will happen
even nearly
& probably that bit
makes me feel
like i have lost
the most.

too sad & too drunk to find my own way home again
i stop at the police station looking for an answer & remember
nothing but my father's number & the recent time i'd shouted
fuck the pigs at a demo outside millbank & ran before the kettle
        *the countless times
i lacked the courage to continue & existed only
on the patient kindness of others whose beds i crawled in:
my mother's at 16 or any boy with stained sheets
        *i didn't fuck
the countless times i stayed awake all night looping
like a gif around the things that made me bad
& told my sister god was dead at bedtime
little heart like an island & a gaping smile
my mum said god's a light inside me & i think
of an exploding bulb a brokenness or just the flat
nothingness i was an expert in lending to the thoughts
or feelings of others sleeping sweet as a pig
& clean of meaning crawling in my bed of mud again

to choose to spend your nasty sour little days with anyone or chew them out alone to burst like rancid bubbles through the neon straw of your perfection: it slackens perspective to even think it, makes my wrists sweat valium thru themselves & the shirt & the jumper & the coat. nothing stops that eager branching of my body out west & east of itself to draw you in *as if i care which way you coil your hose – !* you could take a slice of my luv & not want for weeks but i've eaten the whole & blobby quiche –

sophie please do a better job of yourself
something has been sleeping on your ruins & it barks & whines all night
we are all very tired
take 4x painkillers & turn out the light.

it's the last week of my twenties so why
should i care what the weather does the weather
doesn't give a shit about me   you said
all of this is me shedding my skin before i take
a turn   i imagine myself on the dance floor
of the themed party you won't throw me *o there*
goes that brat again   *she's in her twenties*
but really this year feels more like i'm throwing
up history   & sometimes my life
is too hot to stand up straight in & i want
to run red leggéd down the stairs   but i can't
get out of this tub just wheel
myself from place to place crying & slippery
& a bad thing to look at   how strange & crappy
for you to have to live with my face so often
when for me it's something i glimpse & shed
like a t shirt   or to have to hear me at night
in your ear voice higher & sadder than i
imagined it to be   i do whine like a dog
whenever you go & you do seem always
to be going   keys smashing
on the concrete on the wrong side
of the door   all of this living & waking
is so unbearable   can't find the cold tap
& sleeping feels like drowning
today the light plays us off
against each other   your head's a halo
& i'm all in shadow   & as i slip
into & under the night like a sheet
of paper i will see your face your mouth
opening a great neon silent O
& tomorrow will wake up gasping
wretch white wine into the sink then go
to the nasjonalmuseet & stare at 400 years

of paintings of mountains & midnight sunlight
& buy you a postcard
with a photograph of a bum on it
because i want you to know
i love you
& i am trying to tell you something
& i miss your screaming light

hands flap & roar never normal under wraps & putting on events lest
we get defunded whilst heaving on the nasty pony of our dailiness,
bruised nail beds, visible as babies *no it DISAPPEARS (the body) it goes
away*. i wish it would, rarely, the frontal image of my less good self

a hammer hammering a hammer! ice buckets made of ice! a
cockroach crawling on a rat! a triangle inside a triangle! a chicken
eating KFC! a dog doing an impression of another dog on TV!

you be the rust & I'll be the steel & disappear. you be the rust & I'll be
the steel so get on me. by the shoals on the beach. by the water in its
plenty. by the sheepskin by the chill. by the trains the trains the trains.
by the drowning & the hail. by the moaning by the emails we'll cum
unhooked in time

i've got such a big nose! i should win. i should win an oscar. pissing
in it is the least best way to clean a swimming pool. writing this poem
must be the least best way to say: i like you – all of you – & even though
everything is disappointing & gross, you are all ok the way you are.

do you remember now how the whole place buzzed through
us in the little yellow flat back when our bodies felt cool
& unused: we spooled out light with our hands on
the switch & time moved smoothly (never thrown back
against the wall the red of sharp remembering never thrown
up in a taxi) we got a kitten to replace the mice & he too
trembled on the wires of our lives the burning lines
we sat on waiting to catch fire even after
our best sex was over & the windows became hatches
& the sky turned red at night & we knew who we were
only on certain days & my thighs never ached.
that was one second past the middle of us. i know that now.
with nowhere to go & practically pooping gold
& yellow stars in that shitty flat we got charged
& charged for. i could count this out forever.
i miss you. i guess i'll see you soon.

HURTFACE

i come home late like a man like a stranger zebra headed & foreign put my key in the door & keen & cry for all my flat old places fall asleep on the keyboard & reblog the universe fuck with my long sad dick every last utensil put on whiskey & strip in the garden have a scratchy fight w/next door's pets eat & vom the flowers flowering on my face the face of my stupidness today

listen: i sing when i work & i work all the time with lovely wifi & a sharp clean sharpie & my big girl knickers all in a twist around my throat. i have drawn you a face to wear & it is my face & it hurts me. but whatever now you've come thru the door & in your own face with your job & a bag full of food – o bum! o joy! o bloated world! what dreams i am on the stairs of!

II

if anything gets to be a drag then drop it: clothes. hair. shoes. teeth.
zoos. bubblegum. marx brothers movies. soul music. sci fi. detective
fiction. sunbathing. snowmobiling. walking fast or running slowly.
gathering signatures for a political petition. swimming, golfing & yoga
can be thirsty work. answering a few emails. bridge. macramé is thirsty
the opera is thirsty work. tropical fish are always thirsty. volunteering
for any kind of activity is thirsty work. cabinet making is thirsty.
needlework is thirsty work. baseball is thirsty. writing is very thirsty.
singing is thirsty sealing envelopes for a church mailing list is thirsty
crossword puzzles. cooking. birdwatching is thirsty. amateur acting is
thirsty. leathercraft. gardening. sailing. the guitar is thirsty. movies are
very thirsty. dancing is such thirsty work. marbles are thirsty. bonsai
are thirsty. watercolours are thirsty. an accordion is thirsty. tabletennis
is thirsty. backgammon equipment. a tape collection is very thirsty.
notes for a novel is thirsty. history is always thirsty work. maths is
thirsty. archeology. anthropology is thirsty work.

a hamburger is thirsty honey is thirsty peanuts are thirsty raw
vegetables are thirsty cheese is thirsty cold shrimp are very thirsty
fruit gelatin a mint rape suicide domestic violence divorce is thirsty
work child abuse fierce rage is always thirsty poverty is thirsty hunger
is thirsty illness. injustice is thirsty work.

& love is thirsty love is dirty & not finished thirst is dirty & unfinished
& love is thirsty & love is thirsty work & work is thirsty work is dirty &
not finished love is dirty & unfinished & dirt is dirty dirty is thirsty &
unfinished & thirst is dirty thirst is work & work is thirsty & work is
thirsty & not finished & is thirsty thirst is dirty & not finished & dirt is
lovely dirt is lovely & unfinished & dirt is work & work is lovely & work
is lovely & unfinished & thirst is lovely & love is thirsty & unfinished &
love is work & work is thirsty & lovely & love is lovely & love is lovely &
unfinished & love is thirsty & love is thirsty & love is thirsty work

love is thirsty love is thirsty & unwilling thirst is nervy & unwilling love is fearful & unwilling & fear is thirsty fear is thirsty & forgiving love is thirsty & forgiving & thirst is lovely thirst is lovely & forgiving thirst is nervy & forgiving & nerves are living nerves are living in the writing & writing's thirsty writing's thirsty & unwilling & writing's lovely writing's lovely & forgiving & love is frightening love is frightening & dirty & dirt is lovely dirt is lovely & forgiving & love is nervy & unwilling & will is thirsty will is thirsty & will is thrilling & thirst is frightening thirst is frightening & thirst is living & living's lovely living's lovely & forgiving & love is working love is working & forgiving & work is thirsty, work is nervy & unwilling & work is lovely work is nervy & thrilling & thrill is thirsty & lovely & love is thirsty & love is thirsty & love is thirsty work

& love is ugly & love is ugly love is ugly & lawless snaps my mind shut
thirst is ugly and lawless snaps my mind my mind is ugly my thirst is
ugly takes me some place love takes me some place fancy makes me
thirsty & love is big & early love buys me a drink tells me to sit pretty
thirst tells me to sit pretty & my drinks are pretty ugly snap my mind
& shut me someplace fancy & love me someplace ugly & drink me
someplace lovely & snap me shut with a shallow clap & lock me til i'm
pretty & shut me til i'm lovely & love me til i'm thirsty

& love is thirsty love is dirty & not finished thirst is dirty & unfinished
& love is thirsty & love is thirsty work & work is thirsty work is dirty &
not finished love is dirty & unfinished & dirt is dirty dirty is thirsty &
unfinished & thirst is dirty thirst is work & work is thirsty & work is
thirsty & not finished & is thirsty thirst is dirty & not finished & dirt is
lovely dirt is lovely & unfinished & dirt is work & work is lovely & work
is lovely & unfinished & thirst is lovely & love is thirsty & unfinished &
love is work & work is thirsty & lovely & love is lovely & love is lovely &
unfinished & love is thirsty & love is thirsty & love is thirsty work

i'm not dressed for anything
in my thirsty life dreaming
cooking you bacon & eggs
like a cowboy
                    that's you
meanwhile texting
my therapist
obscure emojis
i used to think i loved parties
where the thirst
came early
but today i like denial
crouching in the corner
of the bed like a present
waiting to be opened
or balancing on one foot
waiting for the coffee pot
the grains sparkling on the hob
the day as long & open
as my inbox

don't remember going downstairs saying sorry or
nevermind just the moment of waking not knowing
if it's dusk or dawn sweating like a hothouse
flower red & wet & pulled up from under & gasping
steeped & steaming like a teabag & drunk on sleep
& beer & sadness blue & dewy as a hothouse
flower & the white white vodka crouching neat
as a bullet low inside me & burning
light like a living laser & i feed it – milk & bread
& honey & lamb – until i'm sticky as an ant
& shining like a hothouse flower thrumming
with the urgent clag of honey blood across
my chest in uneven lubbing – my vodka
heart trembles like a chiahuahua & bruises
break across my skin all purple & yellow
as hothouse flowers & the white hot vodka stars
at dusk & dawn glitter inside me i am beautiful
as a hothouse flower when i turn myself on i light
up in twinkling points between the milky
bones of my ribs & pelvis & all the bulbs
i planted in my fat hot head burst into bright
flowers through my eyes & my teeth bleat
like a lamb & i spark myself up into
a column of coloured light & fire myself
off like a gun going downstairs
to say sorry, nevermind

it's a cold bad night to go out knifing but my baby life has asked me nicely
it's a bad cold night to go out knifing but my baby life has asked me nicely
with your knife you halve the rabbit to split your baby life
with your knife you halve the rabbit the rabbit eat your blade
with your hands you halve the rabbit fat & bone & marrow
with your hands you halve the rabbit pull the socket make it wave
with your knife you halve it nicely cut the blood in jellied slices
bang jump the rabbit call me baby the rabbit call me daddy
bang jump the rabbit in the past bang jump i told you cut
the things that interest me the things that make me glad
it's a cold bad night to go out knifing but you halve the baby twice
i asked you nicely make me sad & call me daddy halve the rabbit
bang jump the night i asked you nicely
the night i asked you nicely
i asked you nicely

my sister takes me to the woods *place the snare along a path* my sister
takes me home to love my sister my rabbit trembles in a trap my
mother leaves down a long path *rabbits are neither strong nor big* my
sister whimpers on the stairs *drive small stakes of wood into the ground*
my mother laughs like it's friday *twist the end of the wire in on itself four
or five times* my sister rents the same video my sister laughs like it's
saturday my father loves me to the fountain to the great steps to the
bandstand once a fortnight my sister drops her ice cream *struggling
will only tighten the noose more around the neck of the rabbit* my sister
pukes in the car my mother pukes out the driver's side door *two small
sticks placed in an x at the foot of the trap* my father tall as a sunflower
my sister's feet at my head her long rabbits toes *mark the location of
the snare with red fabric* my careful sister crimping her hair the shadow
of a threat my stepdad's orange van *rabbits have a lot of predators* the
whole house aflame my mother bent double the bunny clutched to my
chest *rabbits have a lot of predators* to match the beat & for weeks the
smell of charcoal & the fireman's foam dried to a crust on my books
my gifts my mother's jumpers my brother a little eyeless curl of skin
inside her *rabbits have a lot of predators so they are always looking for
a place to hide –*

the little rabbit never recovered from the fire that winter *your hole
should be several feet deep & several feet wide* my red school jumper
chewed clean through as i held him waiting for his cage to be cleaned
*the deeper the hole the lesser the chance the fallen rabbit could climb back
out* we hated it so much we'd leave him in his shit & in the summer
maggots hatched *dig a hole & cover it with sticks* that rabbit hated us &
we were secretly glad when it died the next winter *place the bait in the
very centre so the rabbit's sure to fall* the whole house revving like an
engine each night i used to pray *i'm sorry i didn't like you flopsy but i'm
unhappy too so fuck you*

"I WANT ANOTHER WORLD WHERE WE CAN
BE TOGETHER & HAVE EVERYTHING WE WANT"

my ex says stop using my feelings as material for your work *ima jerk
ima jerk* i know already half out the door wondering how to use this
feeling up & fast pack the kitchen into pieces in phenomenological
disbelief at the ignorance of others re: the particulars of how i live:
where does the kettle go or the plates in a mismatched stash in the
wrong corner of the cupboard.

this is my world i wanna say but no i cannot claim it, rented artex w/a
spatter of mould & no love for thirty years i think of this house & the
inside of your body & wash it for six months in vodka & black air until
i'm sad enough to give up. like a tree in a rock.

stroke my armpits soft as a pet to convince myself i'm clean & have no
secret places am not dying in slow motion or life on pause between
two frames to bring me back from the grave & am not paid to rewind.
i am not the rabbit i am not the butcher i did not jump i did not –

happy valentines i am not
at my jazziest   matching sweat
shirt   hair in a cheerful pony so dirty
it would stay up by itself   "i hope
you're as good at sucking dick
as you are at being lonely"   unknown
quantity of poems inside me   unknown
quantity of living moments   moon's outside
almost full   blood on my pillow
never these days
i take care of myself okay
like a baby something
like a mama something
& my eyes
dressed like candy
big as the moon
& it's fine to be full
of pretty much anything
just for a while i love life i love being
alive one day after another
forever. what's next.

i'm doing my usual but nobody is into it today. i'm not into it. the rabbits aren't into it. i don't know how to become it so i do an impression of it: knock on the door, say hello – i mean it's fine –

what i'm trying to say is i was sick for so long i walked into heaven. jumped around.

CENTURY EGG

i never knew i had the capacity
to make such a cheerful event of my life.

i was raised in the continental style on watered wine
& stayed inside so long my head hurt like a knife
in the garden after a fight
& the stump of the dog's fourth leg
his sharp pink dick his whimper his drooling lockjaw
i've always run up stairs
like i'm being chased   banged my legs
against our fence to test out love & later
plucked out my pubes one by one until my life
became a dream & i was a smooth small girl under the sheet

i could hear the shouting in my sleep
my mother a mystery to me
her love as strong as anger seeping into the thick beams
that held the house up
& if she got too sad she'd throw up
& the air would crackle through the room
& stand our hair on end
her love as loud & sudden as a thunderclap
& the dog whimpering & drooling under the table
& my sister whimpering & drooling on the stairs
& the dinner burning slowly in the oven

III

my razor's swimming
to the bottom
of my bath like a straight
orange fish. i am:
well oiled dirty
& thinking of you. last
night i went to an airport
ate a donut
& fell asleep
on a plane.
i did not disappear
i woke up on the other side
of everything.
the pilot spoke to me
through a machine
& told me it was his last
flight after 22 years
of working for this same
airline. we all clap
very hard. the sun
just pours & pours. i know
exactly who i am. i am
a hole in the ground. waiting
to get full. listening
for my time. you do something
every day
in public. i dance with a dog
& then i kiss you. in the middle
of the street. i suddenly think:
why not just
be happy.

friday night alone
my noodles wobbling in a bowl
body just a grooving
ball of flesh
from room to room
carving a pattern
every city
has an empty place
for me to avoid
being myself in
imagine a different life
no matter what
i'm a perfect offering to god
a pure & gentle meme
. capable of miles & miles
of love
& steadyhearted
grace
my mum didn't always know
she wanted a baby
my whole life
could have been avoided
just imagine
a different kind of happiness
relaxing into the stars
i've worked so hard
if i was never born
i wouldn't lift a finger
could just hang out
singing cosmic karaoke
with whoever
every little thing
with you
recently

has been weirdly
perfect & chaste
i've been busy
fattening myself up
in a sorority of clouds
getting ready for your love
is p much all i do now
& buying cute trousers
in anticipation of summer
the bubbling city air
is only getting hotter
josh sends me a video
from san francisco
a pug is running fast
in dolores park
filthy & panting
their hearts are too big
for their bodies
under sunlight every
body is so ready
to have an experience
makes me think
we were brave
to fuck in winter
the very first
time around

sunshine suddenly today is unbelievable everybody
walking around in it like they've just been born
i do know god but we're not close.
i'm writing porn dialogue for sensitive couples:
don't douche today i love you like you are.
see! it's easy to be me, if you're interested.
just pick something you love & move in with it
immediately. just find something you like doing & ruin it
by doing it forever   it doesn't matter
how you come to know a thing, only that you know
it. i cum tragically at the moment with a kind of sob & all
at once, it's like spilling a drink   *i'm so sorry*   i think this shirt
is too cool for me like it sometimes says *i'll wear sophie today*
& the rest of the time smokes cigarettes in my wardrobe
& being a total bitch to me in front of my jeans. i'm so tired but
i'm not cute enough to wear pyjamas well in front of people
so i put on my fake silk kimono & act natural. it would be nice to kick
back once in a while like a fugly mofo. i'm degraded
from so much wanting & it feels really nice actually. i'm so
unboned from my wanton & deliberate care for you
you can smell me from the hallway. from across
the ocean. the school of my life is stupid & unknowable
& so are you & i love you my paranoid clit bobbing up
& down on thin air like a jet like a tin can. i want to fuck you
in your shirt & tie & i want to hear you say *croissant*. i want
to piss on your thighs. not sure why. but i want you to tell me
to do it & then tell me to do it again & then i do it.
i'm bowled over by your generosity & your smallness
the smell of your hair. i want to write a poem like this
& then write it again but make it more like this
more awkward more bad & more itself.
i want to know a thing so well it makes me sick
i want to love a thing so often it disappears

i want to run around & run around until i get to lie down
i want to bark the name of anything until i pass out

stuck on a loop of the new on a loop of the
moving soundtrack of my singularity
                                  black cherry. sour cherry.
                                  black cherry. sour cherry
i like to drink buckets of anything
& if i smoke a cigarette i'll smoke it until
it's gone. spoil my memory of the cherry
by eating the stone, the stalk. i don't watch
porn just flicker off & on to some
abstracted memory of it: some
body bent double like a horse in a cage
a public pool rimmed with cum. wet cement.
faded jeans. black forest. cherry chocolate.
i want to text you
a picture of my dinner   to show you
what's moving around
inside me.   wet cement. faded jeans.
sour cherry. black forest.
wet cement. sour cherry.
faded jeans. my dreams are clouded
not pictures just the feelings of pictures
tense pitch. dawn rim. black forest
ghost warden. sour sour cherry
sour cherry. black chocolate.
wet cement. wet cement.
don't mistake my message
for its content: i've got nothing
to tell you   i just wanted
to be in touch.

god between my trees god bouncing up & down
not light itself but a type of light
us lying head to head
cherry white cherry
white chewing gum
stretched back & forth
like string talking
not light but light's bouncing
why does everything last this way
dreaming in a time of war
call my ex for no reason just to feel warm
paedophiles in the academy defended silently
rapists in the academy defended loudly
an impossible account of emotional labour at the movies
a yellow puppy in your jacket snoring gently
god between my trees bouncing round & round
no apparatus no bell to ring
just string talking
in my dream we laughed until i almost peed
lungs bouncing in & out like trees
should i text you that
no
kellyanne conway kneeling on a couch
like a god
empty
like a feminist t-shirt
on etsy
you
kneeling on a bed
like a god made in china
kneeling under a tree
pink clouds in my toilet
nobody's baby
just cherry

blossoms rolling
off a string of blood
an arc of urine
bending like light
when a tree moves
i might

there are places in which the mind thrives like plankton, where jobs
are easy to come by & every apartment overlooks the park, where
the funeral has barely started & the heart is a mist that rises & clears
like a browser & streaming faster – a gapless surface of fake solids

& there are places in which love reproduces itself like a lizard's tail, heeds
to no alarm or database. places where the sun raises like a fat cunt
glowing in the sky. places where the rats don't race but rat out
their days in a waterlogged stupor. places you can dive into from a height

there are places where a heart is megashared & its kitchens always full
of foods. where babies name themselves. a place you cannot unknow
& in some place from the past there is a bucket doubling as a womb, full
of infant newts & frogspawn. in some place you cannot know is you

full to the brim with ungendered yearning. & there are places that smell
of honey and decay, places where mistakes can be undone by pressing
a sequence of two or three keys. places where the language flows uncoded,
where everybody understands each other. there are places where people

burn money to keep warm, places where every shop window is broken
    & blood
makes patterns on the walls. there are places where every building looks
the same & nothing can be bought or sold. there are places through which
a tall fence runs with holes too small to kiss your opposite number

& there are places in which each citizen is tattooed, head to toe,
    with the face
and body of another citizen & everybody takes to the lakes naked, places
where public transport is free & police tip their hats to beggars
    on the streets
& nobody dies. there are places where the dead rise from their graves

& avenge the living, places where the dead turn into doves just to peck
themselves dead again. there are places in which bleeding takes the place
of talking, places with water in place of mirrors, with eyes instead of
    cameras,
patches of pure darkness on a google map, places you can't arrive or leave

& there are places in which the lives of happy and boring people unfold
day after day, where nobody writes anything down & nobody suffers
from the damp & cold. there are places you have been & will
never go again, where the yearning to visit stands in for the visiting

as though you could trick yourself out of death or labour for a second
go at being free. there are places where the moon is god-blocked into
a pinprick, & places where it largens & honeys, places night never falls
& the citizens sleep with snakes across their eyes to block the light

& the heart itself a snake knotted into a place we can never see or fathom
a stupid fist raised in protest, shrinking by the minute, longing to be
    dropped
in steaming water, to expand to the size of a glass like a hybrid tea rose
    sewn
together in a factory in bangladesh & sold for eight hundred times its
    worth

& the workers streaming utopia their bodies dropping from the walls all
    night

& if i took my clothes off tonight the stars might all fall out of the sky

loving u is an amazing invention i never knew exists

diet coke bottle with ur name on it says i could win a holiday to
    heaven

this new sadness is wholly mine & i feel pretty safe inside it

i just can't get on board with the cuteness of living today

as the plane pulls my body from the earth it's easy to forget

i'm just a bag of tenderness of blood & dirty water

chasing a new moon dusk across the atlantic my thigh pressed to a
    stranger

so much of this earth is just moon & water

so much of this earth is just silver

so much of my life is just watching life being lived

potato chip crumbs

tylenol pm

a stunning list of frank sinatra's lovers

my hairdresser believes that two years ago we entered a parallel
    universe

almost but not quite the same as the one before it

& i so easily buy that

everything's wrong & good & ample

everything's a cartoon of devastation

i flew so high then crashed back to earth like it was no big deal

in the middle of london there's a burned out monument of bodies

& fire is so unreal

two pink gummy bears fucking on my couch

jeremy corbyn sniffing a red rose

jeremy corbyn cutting a chocolate brownie cake into slices

on instagram i can see that u are somewhere still meditating

a sound from the diaphragm forced up thru the throat

the radicalisation of young white men

i find ur face & silence frightening

love is just a drive-by in the dark with all the windows wound right
    down

found myself pressed naked to a wall two fingers pressed to my anus

in the apartment of a honeysweet stranger

do u like this do u want it

standing with one leg on the bed getting fucked to r&b in a lazy heat

net curtain waving on the breeze

& i remember how to be the good meat

for a while

but it's no use

i'm dead without speaking or being spoken to

bucket of creamy coffee screaming on my desk like a preacher

american doors are hard to open you have to shoulder thru

the effort of my thoughts as one long poem breaking in

late at night in london the dead are burning still

the dead are listening

the dead are poor & angry

the new moon is just the same old moon cutting back across itself

i knew this already

i willed it to be so

when you turn
32 the planets of the lovers
are in the exact same place
in the sky as they were
when you were born
mars return
venus return
when you went away
i only kept quiet when i ate
do i not even now
have something in my mouth
as i write this
a gummy void   a baby void
my consolations
because i was lovehungry –
when you return
like the moon curving the earth
don't call me
by my name
my milky folds
my pinky folds
my moony face   o this trance im in
i leave myself on read
take a white bath
shave my legs to the top
consult the mystics of youtube
from the tub
nothing lasts forever
so stay a little hungry
so let the void stay empty
so let the moon sway gently
as it comes round the corner
my eyes get stuck on aurora –

everything returns   so i don't have to
moon now reflected
in a wide & round   reservoir of milk
down at the edge of town
further from the sun now   my winter of bad thots
my life in black tshirts   i left me on read again
so i stay a little empty   took off my tshirt again
so i stay a little hungry   a little further from the sun again
so im watching that same film again
so im eating my same feelings again:
pop tart   peanut buttercup
marshmallow shishkabob
          cheeseball pickmeup

                    nothing lasts forever
                    white ladies! sing to me:
     lorelai gilmore
            rory gilmore
                    cher
                              christina ricci
        winona ryder
                         madonna
                         madonna
                    madonna
            hi mama
        return

some nights i cant bear the sex & lying flat can barely reach the light
& then these days i suck my pen off flick my nips grind against the
    desk
staring at my inbox
who am i
where do the days go
a slice of my life fried in blue light
& diazepam piled up on every surface of my home
& a bath
so hot i burn my clit off
so hot i pass out

> *understand me*
> *i never said i wasn't late to love*
> *wasn't crazy*
> *you know i die*
> *you know i die*

& the rabbit passed out from too much talking
& the rabbit passed out from too much tender rabbiting
& then the rabbit was so sad
& then the rabbit was so sad

>   *understand me*
>   *you already know what you have to do*

you're drunk rabbit go home

>   *you already know what you have to do so do it*

& my cat hangs his head over his meat in a juicy prayer
& my cat comes home with a rabbit in his jaw
& my cat licking himself out slowly on the bed at dawn
you're drunk cat go home

>   *you already know what you have to do so do it*

>   *thanks. yeah let's let go. x* go home

rabbit you're so sweet rabbit you're so sweet
spiking my life in lit moments from a blanket of dust
spiking my fur in small tufts from a blank sheet of us

blanket you're so drunk go home

thanks. yeah let's let go. x go home

some nights i cant bear the bed & i sleep on the floor
bumper sticker in the driveway says *honk if ur heartsick then honk for
  more*

rabbit you're so sweet
i'm stuck on your beautiful memes
rabbit you're an angel keep on living
rabbit you're an angel keep on living

some nights i cant bear the thought & i sleep on all fours
farming emails in my dreams & pounding walls
bumper sticker in the driveway says *on the 31st January 2017*
a mass deportation charter flight is set to remove
up to 100 people from the UK to Nigeria and Ghana
honk if ur heartsick then honk for more

coffee
please please understand me
late at night & in a cosmic waistband
my hand on your chest was the rabbit itself
& i turned down the light to just tell you
you make me happy
you make me happy
please understand
rabbit you're sosososo
caffeine free vanilla diet coke   *thanks. yeah let's let go. x*

some nights i go home
bumper sticker on my driveway says *i want too much of everything*
life is dripping down the sides of itself
imagine your fist in me
imagine bringing back waterboarding

some nights i lie down outside in the fucked up sun
rabbit you were never a clown get up
bumper sticker on my driveway says *donald trump*

& the rabbit passed out because the rabbit was drowning
& the rabbit passed out because the rabbit was drowning

rabbit were you born this way
rabbit you're so drunk
rabbit you're so drunk go home

there are men everywhere
men with no apparent qualification
every time i see a man i feel sadder
& it makes my life worse

bumper sticker on my mirror says *synthetic sweetness made you sick*
bumper sticker on my mirror says *hmu if ur dtf*
bumper sticker on my driveway says *i dont want to see myself in anybody
else's art i don't want to know what they think they know about me i dont
want magic i just want silence sitting on the special step halfway up &
full of love & known by no-one i don't want to get drunk i just want to get
fucked up i don't want to get drunk i just want to get fucked up i don't want
to be understood i just want to eat all your food & care about you & control
my moods & stop deportation &*

some nights i'm what's inside the egg that's hatching in the neck
of the snake & sliding down easy street knowing what i know
some nights i'm on tv
& some nights really i just get in the way of myself

my friends holding each other aloft in the flood
please don't deport my friends
let them go home let them get drunk
don't let me go
don't let me i want to eat the weather
i want to eat the sound of everything falling apart
i want the snow to come down thick as the day is long
i want to name something inside me then squirt it out on the bed in
      fits of sad desire
it's hard not to kill yourself in times of crisis
bumper sticker on my mirror says *bounce back hard*
bumper sticker on my mirror says *open borders*

i wish i never had to shut my mind to love
don't let me go let my friends get drunk
caffeine free vanilla diet coke please don't
let my friends die in the flood
please let my friends get drunk
in the snow in the thickening if ur my friend
you can call me any time you need me
& i will listen even if life made you mean
i wish i never had to shut my mind to love

just because you feel like trash doesn't mean you're trash
just because you're sad doesn't mean you have to show
everyone your sadness like it's the news

*just because capitalism makes everything trash doesn't mean that words
and images aren't real and important. we are both the damage we do to
ourselves and others and the possibility of more than this*

what's left
i know you love the porn but i think it holds you back
& i just want you to know
in your fat serenity   in your ordinary difficulty
in your personal hotspots of self-triggering
in your medication against an intolerable reality
how much i vibe with you
i could build a heaven for your soft head
touch my belly   tell me to be someone

the water bounces off the grease in the pan
no matter how hot i run it
you want me to talk about god well i can
god is just a facemask
eternity wears
strings of yolk, an earwig, the sweet
corn blocking the outlet pipe
a boat ride to ikea
dollar slice of pizza with erica
a feeling that things will get better
ive been walking on the moon i tell you
& space is full of happy ghosts
wearing their skins like linens
warbling, loose weaved
if there are 7.6 billion
people on earth there
are 100x times
more than that
in space
we always think that we are where it's at
                        life's persistence
is pretty wild
the eyes of animals at night
wherever i am & everywhere else as well
the widening of the street
o folding back of sadness
frameless –
                        the steady kind of gorgeous
we find in the newly born & the divine

EDWARD SCISSORHANDS

all the tragic animals eating in their meadows
like balloons full of water
their sudden lives bursting around a fist
there's a hole in my chest like a punched wall
ceremonial fires are lit & left to burn
everybody's so unmended these days
it breaks my heart
a fist clenching around eternity
blue blood   blue light
black yellow bruises cross the sky
i do long to be covered over
muzzled
there's nothing here for me
in this feeling
the finest tip of this feeling touching
my brain blooms out like pen on wet paper
god has stopped speaking to me
pen clenched in my fist
i burst across god
like a busted waterbed
a river of god
edward scissorhands
i remember his monster shame
the way he cut up everything he loved
the way the way we are can make us an enemy to our tenderness
sophie you don't have to take it all so seriously
hot wet god
the shame of being known
dadbod jesus bloated on a beach
i want to take care of you / i want to take care of me
dadbod jesus on his knees
edwards scissorhands crying at the party
dadbod jesus watching over me

ducking my head under each wave on fire
island i try to think of other times ive felt this done
w/life & survived
frank o'hara died here everybody knows
alcoholics die everywhere all the time everybody knows
he was purple wherever his skin showed
      i never thought of myself as a useless drunk
          i never felt
so unspecial   *through the white hospital gown*
in the daytime it feels
like it would be easy to die
to dip my head under
         just a second too long
           but in the dark death is real
   like an animal up close
            he was a quarter larger than usual
on the edge of sleep you could fall
straight into & thru it   & nobody wld know yr name there
naked in the atlantic at midnight cutting a path where the moon hits
the water i could swim a straight line out into forever & nobody
would stop me. would know my name. *every few inches*
there was some sewing composed
of dark blue thread i want to shut my eyes i want to shut a million things
strawberry moon   orange to silver   my simple tits
bobbing on the water   *some stitching was straight and three or four*
inches long   *others were longer and semicircular*   urge to die
  breathing out & folding in
on itself until it feels like nothing we get out shiver lose the keys
  to the house
find them & laugh on the porch   *the lids of both eyes were bluish black*
  jameson
drinking an inch of mezcal & me sucking on my seltzer like it's a beer
alive   smiling   only half-quitting   only half-gone   a normal
  heart

flashing in & out on the shore *it was hard to see his beautiful*
blue eyes which receded a little into his head   the wifi is out
my 4g is fake   replacing each image in my recent life with a square
    and a ?
(i know rite)   *he breathed with quick gasps. his whole body quivered.*
                        i have taken a solemn vow to stop looking
at your face on the internet   to stop imagining your unkind thoughts
                        of me   my life as a little nobody
there was a tube in one of his nostrils down to his stomach
i go to sleep in a wood-panelled room the same length & width
as my bed   & count the waves as they break
over my head   i sleep like im already dead
                        face to the wall
greedy for the nothing   won't fall
in the crib he looked like a shaped wound
i wake up constipated
in the morning sun   drink coffee & smoke
on the beach feeling full of shit   & good to no-one
his leg bone was broken and splintered and pierced the skin
every rib was cracked.
a third of his liver was wiped out by the impact
i could make a home here prone forever
belly to the sand
let my messages go unread
let my phone battery run flat
let the sun burn my back
let all the ships fuck up on the rocks
indistinguishable baby small   little pieces
floating   like the world floats   gay   unbroken
bloated & golden
a monument to my favourite alcoholic
the greatest homosexual   who ever lived & died

at dusk each day i like to think
of all my new friends in different parts
of the city jerking off   running baths
vaping weed getting sober   running their mouths
   & reading poetry aloud to one another.
alice says i have the right to repeat myself so i do
alice says you can cry if you need to so i do
she looks away   scrolls pictures
of dogs on instagram
& we watch the traffic dancing
towards the bridge
everybody on their way
somewhere
        i want to go far –
jameson says i know u know it will get better
i nod closed mouthed in a gesture i believe to convey quiet bravery
(too little too late)
it's so hot & close u can almost lick the weather's face today
        steam rises off the east river
in a film god kills herself by removing her own intestines
          i don't have the guts to watch it
jameson's poems are so rangey on the bench like a godhead
my mother's arm is broken & strapped to her side on skype
my dad calls me baby in a text when he's drunk
i don't know what this means
            god's suicide scene
at the cinema last night we didn't understand a thing but were so happy
just to be there not on our way
anywhere.   *i want to go far far –*
the film said loving someone was the only thing to do
& in it one of the characters described the music he listened to
as *soupy*   it's a bad translation
cori laughs & made a joke in french. *un soupçon –*
the film begins & ends with a woman covered in blood

& andrew said maybe we are supposed to understand it all backwards
i guess that's how love works too   it's all faith
until the end   & then you see it
later for what it is or wasn't or what it coulda been   the whole trick
when i see your face
or hear your name
i want to pass out
from love
from sadness
from shame
& from regret.
when i arrived
in america
i wished simply
to drown
in feeling & forget
about work
but then i got
so wet
i had to start
swimming.
steam rises off the east river.
john giorno says *it's not what happens it's how you handle it –*
i chew on language here:
philly cheesesteak   rockaway park
taconic state parkway   restroom   sidewalk
              mama i'm so tired
some days i take secret photographs of americana   & feel like a
    normal alien
alice & i talk on a bench whilst the sun sets & watch the lights
in the apartment building opposite turn on
one by one.
last week i drank bourbon & cried
for four nights solid soaking through my sheets
my t shirts & the mattress. over & over.
fevery dream in which i see a drunk
woman (me) doing shots & snorting coke from a key.

i tell her let me help you
& then i open a wound on her arm
& remove from the wound a giant plastic egg.
i crack the egg to reveal a small wooden sphere
& from it emerges a large white rat. don't ask me how.
i put the rat on a leash & walk it back to my apartment.
i go to sleep in my dream petting the rat & wake up feeling good.
i give the rat breakfast which she eats happily.
i kiss her head.
i go back to the bar & find the woman (me) sicker than ever.
thin, sweating, with two black eyes & a purple arm.
i say hey what happened
& she says
you shouldn't have taken what you took the way you took it.
you shouldn't have taken what you took the way you took it.
you shouldn't have taken what you took the way you took it.
i leave her on the floor to die. what do i care. i have my rat.
alice says i have the right to repeat myself so i do.
on the hot drive from hudson cathy gets me to do impressions
of different british accents and describe the city
i come from. when I get back to my apartment
i vomit in the kitchen sink
then the bathroom sink
then the toilet
then again in the shower. pink ribbons of bile & wine.
I am the only person at the john giorno installation
in hell's kitchen on a wednesday afternoon & i cry
for twenty minutes watching him speak on a twenty foot projector
    screen.
thanks for nothing america i did it all without you
i sometimes wish a lesbian could be given this much room. to do
    anything.
you don't love me & the feeling of not being loved comes in waves
                    steam rising off the east river
i kiss my rat's head. i am such a bad peach. seeing it all backwards.
the world is so big! desire alone makes it small
there's nothing funny about being a lesbian today

on my hands & knees like juiced fruit
in prayer position at the gallery the cinema the bathroom floor
you shouldn't have taken what you took the way you took it
when i got back to the apartment the rat was drunk
when i got back to the apartment the rat jerked me off
when i got back to the apartment the rat was me
jameson gets me to stand on stage at the amphitheatre by the river
to take a picture
steam rises
i lose sight of him for a second & it's just me & the water & the bridge
    & the dog
gently pissing   [self help / fake rumi poem says
            only when i quit believing in myself did i come to such beauty]
there's a power in loneliness i need to channel
there's a freedom in not being loved i need to channel
it's not what happens it's how you handle it –
i came to america to be a solid gold flower floating down the river
& now reduced to repeating my own name out loud, my DOB, where
    i live
the things i did today. splashing my face in the kitchen sink over & over
honestly i am sick of helping jesus count days
my mother's limp white arm. the things she gave & took.
                        mama i'm so sad
america begins & ends in blood   *i want to go far far far –*
sometimes i get off on meanness
            the holding back the love that's bucking against the gate
penny arcade says when she came to new york she saw a sign
at a head shop saying
        you are a daughter of the universe
            this city is mine just as much as it's anyones!
today is my 32nd birthday. i wish i had never been born.
andy warhol was a fraud. fame is a kind of violence.
ambition makes me sick. i want to close every door.
i don't care about kathy acker. i don't care about anything anymore.
there's no art in america, it's all sugar & war.
i shouldn't have taken what i took the way i took it   but listen:
wherever in the world

if i never see you again
     always on your way
somewhere   i will love you
     gently
the whole length
of my life
i want nothing
for you
but endless poetry
easy ppl
slow morning
strong coffee
dynamic emoji
time to read
dancing dog
uncracked screen
mountain
bunny
a million years
deep sense of peace
& somebody
who loves you
for free
when she sees
your animal grace
your swagger
the way you open fruit </3
o! i am glad
to have known you
my devastating weakness
my white rat
my river of gold
& my old
     wild
        american
           heart   xxx

ACKNOWLEDGEMENTS

Parts of 'fucking up on the rocks' are taken from Larry Rivers' eulogy for Frank O'Hara, as transcribed by *The New York Times*.

Parts of 'lit moments' are taken from the following sources: a Facebook status by Nina Power, a facebook status by CN Lester, a comment made by CA Conrad in the film *The Book of Conrad* (2016), and Virginia Woolf's *A Room of One's Own*.

The title 'push the soft hem of the night' is taken from Denise Riley's poem 'Wherever You Are, Be Somewhere Else' (Selected Poems, Reality Street, 2000).

'mystics of youtube' contains lines from the 1990 film *Mermaids*.

Parts of 'art in america' are taken from work by Penny Arcade, John Giorno and Tara Brach. Special thanks to Jameson Fitzpatrick for inspiring the title and to Andrew Durbin, Alice O'Malley and Corina Copp for saying cool stuff that ended up in the poem. The film I reference and quote from in the poem is *L'Important C'est D'aimer* (1975).

Versions of these poems have appeared in *BOMB, Lambda Literary, Granta, Poetry Review, Ploughshares, n+1, The White Review, The Brooklyn Rail, Gramma,* and *The Morning Star.*

Thank you to Jack Underwood, Jameson Fitzpatrick, Karen Schaller, Ruth Novaczek, Samantha Walton, Jo Walton, Philip Langeskov, Corina Copp, Emily Berry, Sara Wintz, Ariana Reines, CA Conrad, Eileen Myles, Johanna Linsley, Season Butler, Justin Hunt, Christa Holka, Brian Lobel and many others for supporting my work, providing incredible feedback and believing in me. A special thanks to my editor Nathan Hamilton for making this book the best book it could be.

Thank you to my family – Alan, Jo, Clare, Laura, Tallulah (the original rabbit), Finn, Job, Skye, Dulcie, Irene, Derek, John, Carrie, Eli, Albie, Lynn, JP, Rosalia & William. I love you all very much. & thank you to my friends – my chosen family – for keeping me alive all this time.

Rabbit
By Sophie Robinson

First published in this edition by Boiler House Press, 2018
Part of UEA Publishing Project

Design and typesetting by Emily Benton
emilybentonbookdesigner.co.uk

Typeset in Arnhem
Printed by Imprint Digital, UK
Distributed by NBN International

ISBN 978-1-911343-45-5